Sandra Deneke, Inga Ettelt, Karin Möcklinghoff, Kevin Marc Patterson

Herausgeberin: Sandra Deneke

navi

W0198435

Englisch 5/6

Arbeitsheft 5

1. Auflage, 1. korrigierter Nachdruck 2009

Bestellnummer 61279

Bildungsverlag EINS

Haben Sie Anregungen oder Kritikpunkte zu diesem Produkt?
Dann senden Sie eine E-Mail an 61279_001@bv-1.de
Autoren und Verlag freuen sich auf Ihre Rückmeldung.

Grafik: Marlene Pohle, Stuttgart

Umschlaglayout: Astrid Sitz, Köln

Umschlagfoto: picture-alliance

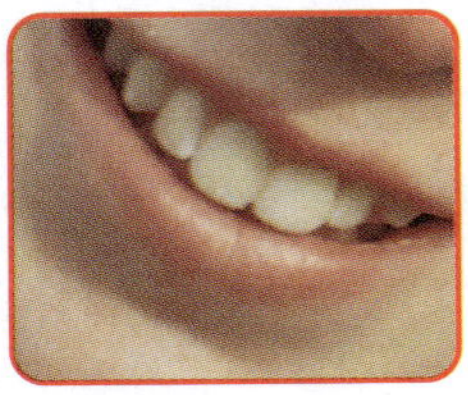

Aufgaben zur Übung der Sprechkompetenz.

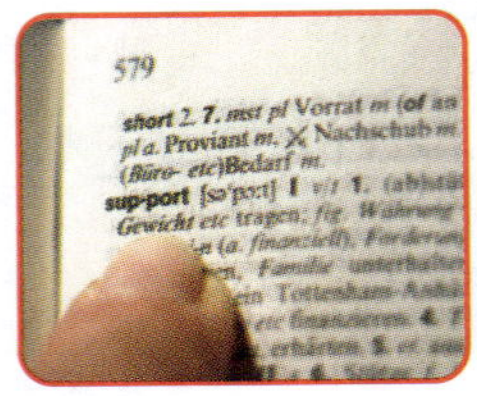

Aufgaben dienen zur Einübung des Wortschatzes.

Aufgaben zur Übung der Schreibkompetenz.

Aufgaben dienen zur Einübung bestimmter grammatikalischer Phänomene.

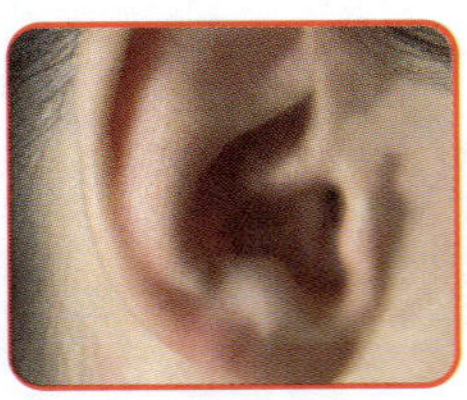

Aufgaben dienen als Hörverständnisübungen.

Dieses Symbol verweist auf weiterführende Aufgabenstellungen für stärkere Schüler.

Aufgaben dienen zur Übung der Lesekompetenz.

Zu diesen Aufgaben liegt ein Text auf der zugehörigen CD vor.

Dieses Arbeitsheft deckt die Kapitel 1–4 sowie den 1. Teil von Kapitel 10 des Schülerbuchs „Navi Englisch 5/6“ ab. Es wird ergänzt durch das Arbeitsheft 6.

www.bildungsverlag1.de

Bildungsverlag EINS GmbH
Sieglarer Straße 2, 53842 Troisdorf

ISBN 978-3-427-**61279**-7

Contents

1	**Welcome to English: I can speak English**	4	
	To go around the world	4	sich über die Weltsprache Englisch austauschen
	Do you know all the countries?	6	Wortschatz: Ländernamen
	How many English words do you know?	7	englische Begriffe
	Vocabulary: Welcome to English	8	mit dem Wörterbuch arbeiten
2	**About me: You and I**	9	
	Greetings	9	Hörverständnis
	Numbers	10	Wortschatz: Zahlen von 1 bis 12
	Number Search	11	Wortschatz: Zahlen von 1 bis 12
	Introductions	12	Informationen aufbereiten
	Interview with my friends	13	sich bekannt machen
	This is my friend	14	Grammar: jemanden vorstellen
	Which pronoun (Fürwort)?	15	Grammar: persönliche Fürwörter
	Vocabulary: About me	16	mit dem Wörterbuch arbeiten
3	**At school: Our classroom**	17	
	What is missing?	17	Wortschatz: Schule
	I like colours	18	Wortschatz: Farbe
	What is this?	19	Wortschatz: Schule
	What colour is your ...?	20	Informationen aufbereiten
	Between the lessons.	21	Hörverständnis
	Vocabulary: At school	22	mit dem Wörterbuch arbeiten
4	**Free time: Sports and hobbies**	23	
	Let us play Bingo	23	Hörverständnis
	Tom's week	24	Hörverständnis
	Tom's hobbies/Some more hobbies	25	Wortschatz: Hobbys
	What are their hobbies.	26	Grammar: like/likes
	Interview about hobbies	27	ein Interview machen
	Vocabulary: Free time	28	mit dem Wörterbuch arbeiten
10a	**Around the year: Christmas – Easter**	29	
	Christmas	29	etwas präsentieren
	Decorations and reading	30	Wortschatz: Weihnachten
	Easter	31	Wortschatz: Farben
	Where is ...?	32	Grammar: Verhältniswörter
	Vocabulary: Around the year	33	mit dem Wörterbuch arbeiten
	Mein Sprachenportfolio	35	

To go around the world

1. Look at the map. In which countries do you speak English?

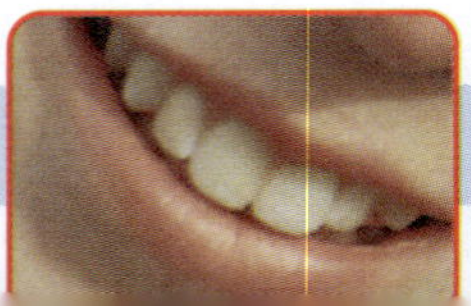

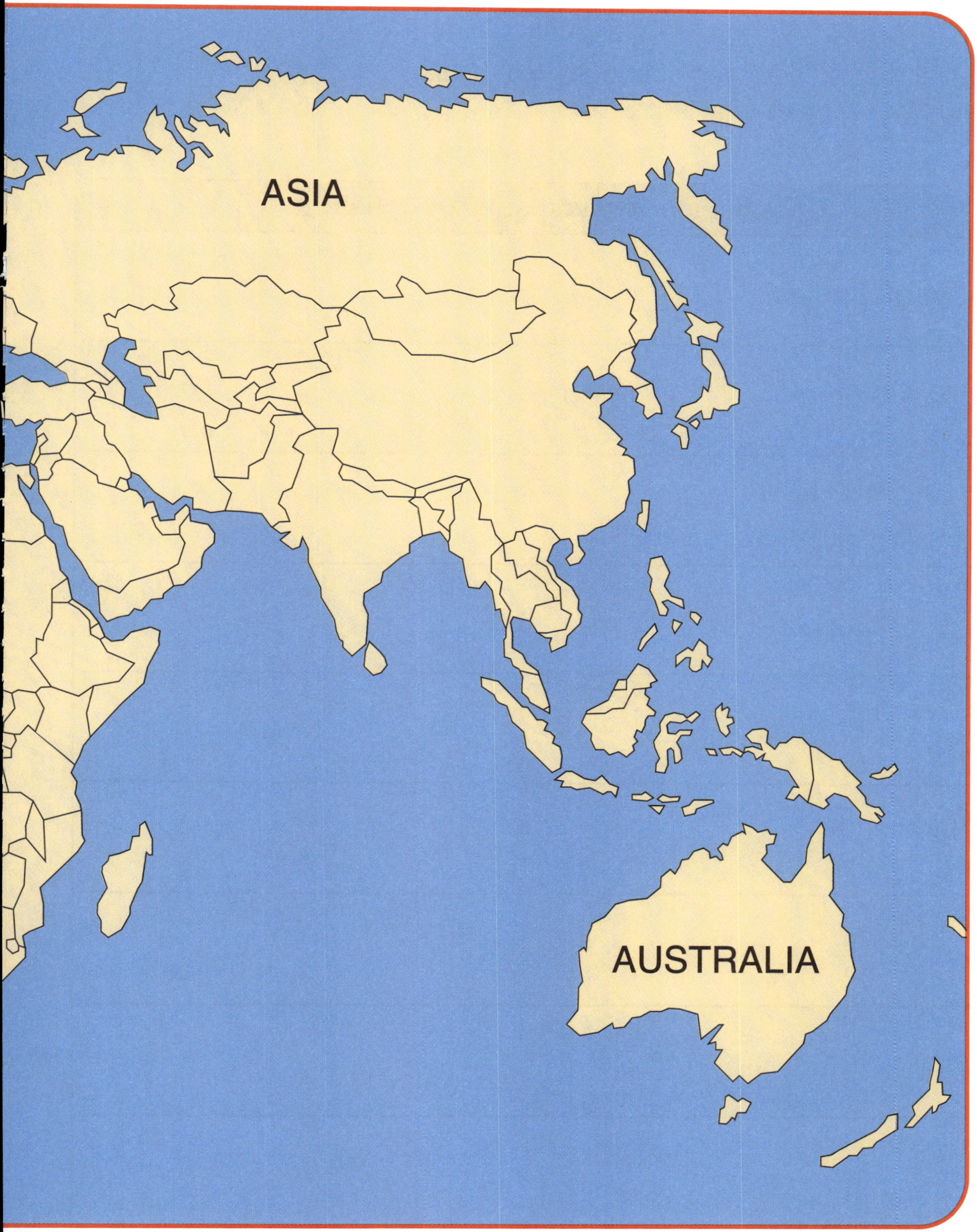

2. Colour the countries in red.

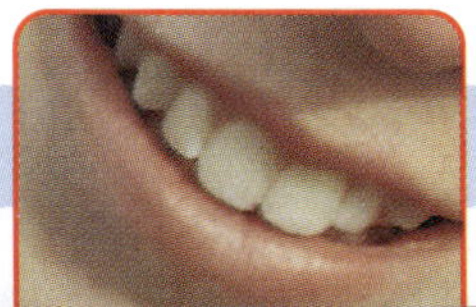

Do you know all the countries?

1. Write all the red coloured countries into the list.

Countries where you speak English	
01	*Great Britain*
02	
03	
04	
05	
06	
07	
08	
09	
10	

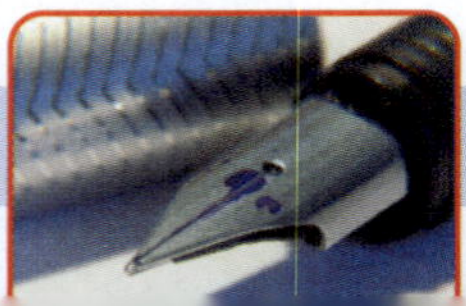

How many English words do you know?

1. Think of English words you know and write them into the list.

clothes	colours	food
	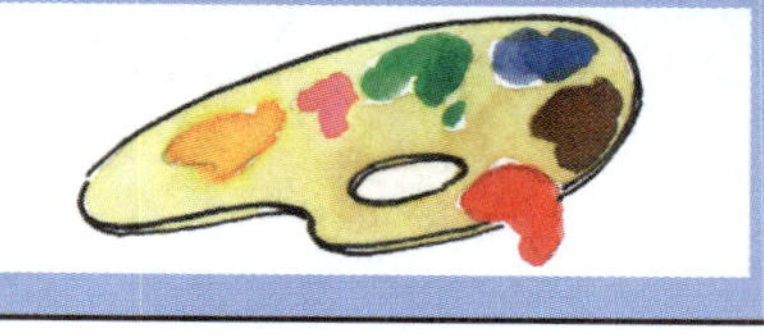	
trousers	red	cheese

2. Draw 5 of the objects from your list. Add the correct word.

Vocabulary: Welcome to English

1. Match the pictures with the correct words. Use your ruler.

an apple

a country

butter

milk

the world

a banana

a map

a pair of jeans

a neighbour

a song

2. Compare with your neighbour. Write the words into the list.

1. ______________________
2. ______________________
3. ______________________
4. ______________________
5. ______________________
6. ______________________
7. ______________________
8. ______________________
9. ______________________
10. ______________________

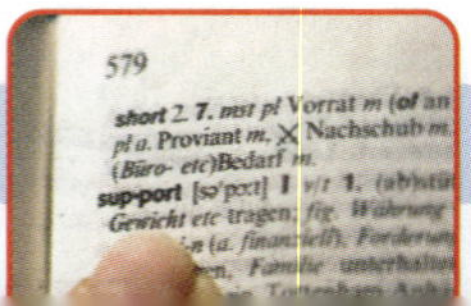

Greetings

Track 04

1. Listen to the CD.
   What do they say?

Hello!

Good morning!

Good morning, boys and girls!

Hi!

Good morning, Mrs. Johnson!

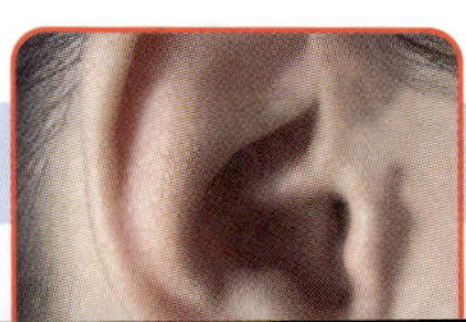

Numbers

1. In the boxes you can find a number.
   Write the number next to the box.

T W O → 2

N T E

L E E N V E

E R TH E

E H I G T

E I V F

O N E

U R O F

S I X

E S N E V

N I N E

W E V E L T

2. Colour the number box and the number line in the same colour.
   Write the number on the correct line.

1 _ _ _	7 _ _ _ _ _
2 _ _ _	8 _ _ _ _ _
3 _ _ _ _ _	9 _ _ _ _
4 _ _ _ _	10 _ _ _
5 _ _ _ _	11 _ _ _ _ _ _
6 _ _ _	12 _ _ _ _ _ _

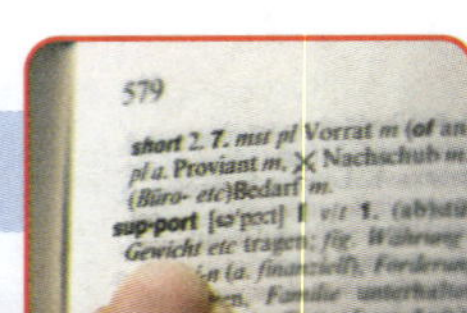

Number Search

1. Find the numbers from 1 to 12 in the grid. → ↓ ↑
   Take a marker and colour the boxes.
2. Write the numbers on the lines in the correct order (from 1 to 12).

T	W	E	L	V	E	F	S
H	E	N	R	D	L	I	I
R	T	W	O	Z	E	V	X
E	U	G	S	E	V	E	N
E	V	B	L	O	E	N	N
F	O	U	R	N	N	I	R
V	Y	F	T	E	A	N	M
E	I	G	H	T	I	E	O

1 O N E

2 _ _ _

3 _ _ _ _ _

4 _ _ _ _

5 _ _ _ _

6 _ _ _

7 _ _ _ _ _

8 _ _ _ _ _

9 _ _ _ _

10 _ _ _

11 _ _ _ _ _ _

12 _ _ _ _ _ _

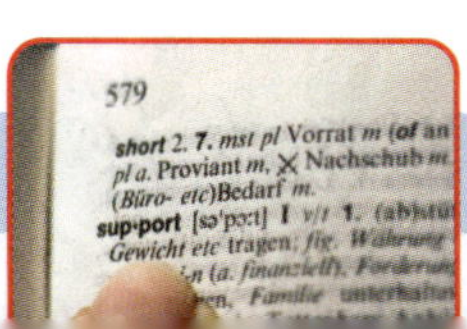

Introductions

1. Look into your textbook and find the information.
   And what about you? Fill it in:

				**YOU**
name				
age				
city				

2. Now introduce yourself:

Hello, my name is ______________________

______________________________________.

I am ______________________________

______________________________________.

I am ______________________________

______________________________________.

3. Make a poster and hang it up in your classroom.

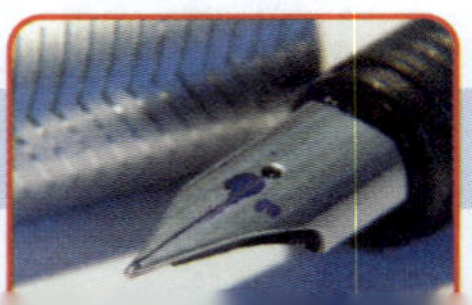

Interview with my friends

1. Draw a line from the question to the correct word.

How old are you?

Where are you from?

What is your name?

name

age

city

2. Now ask five friends and write their answers into the table.

	name	age	city
1			
2			
3			
4			
5			

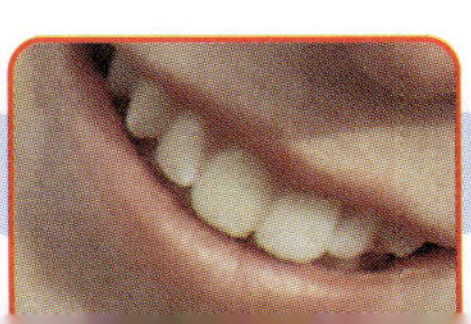

This is my friend

1. Draw a picture of your friends into the boxes:

This is ______________________.

__________ is ______________________.

__________ is from __________________.

______________________________.

______________________________.

______________________________.

2. Put this into the correct order. Colour the pairs in the same colour. Write the pairs on the line.

I are
you is
he are
she are is
it is
we
you am
they are

I am ______________________

____

____

____

____

____

____

____

Which pronoun (Fürwort)?

1. Fill in the right word.

I

he

I

she

you

2. Find another word.

Sally is new.	______ is new.
Paul and Emily are from Bristol.	______ are from Bristol.
My T-shirt is new.	______ is new.
Paul is a boy.	______ is a boy.

you

he

I

we

you

she

it

they

Vocabulary: About me

1. Match the pictures with the correct words. Use your ruler.

a card

a book

a boy

a girl

a name

a word

a city

a number

a teacher

twelve

2. Compare with your neighbour. Write the words into the list.

1. ______________________________
2. ______________________________
3. ______________________________
4. ______________________________
5. ______________________________
6. ______________________________
7. ______________________________
8. ______________________________
9. ______________________________
10. ______________________________

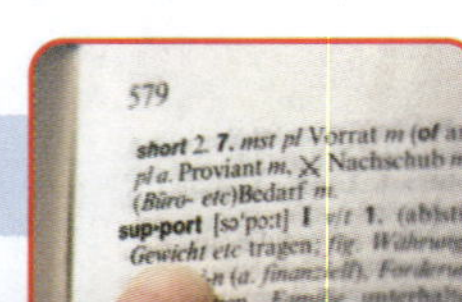

What is missing?

1. Continue the serial. Speak, draw and write.

pencil ______ ______

glue ______ ______ ______

timetable ______ ______

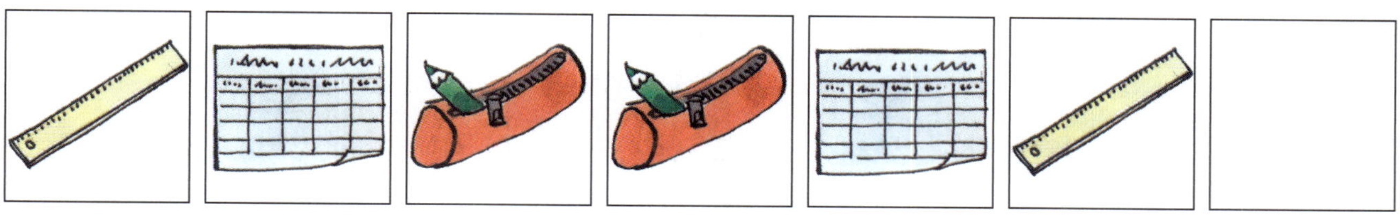

ruler pencil-case ______ ______

folder ______ ______

schoolbag ______ ______ ______

2. Make your own puzzle.

______ ______ ______ ______ ______

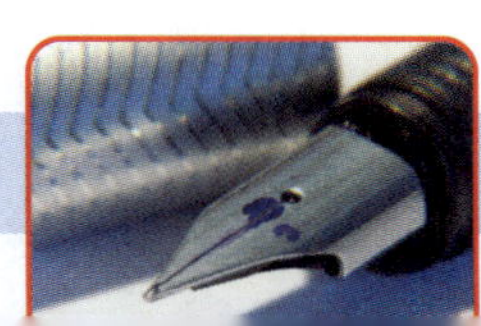

I like colours

1. Mix your own colours.
2. Colour a small piece of paper.
3. Cut it out and glue.
4. Write down the name of the new colour.

blue and yellow =

____

blue and red =

____

yellow and red =

____

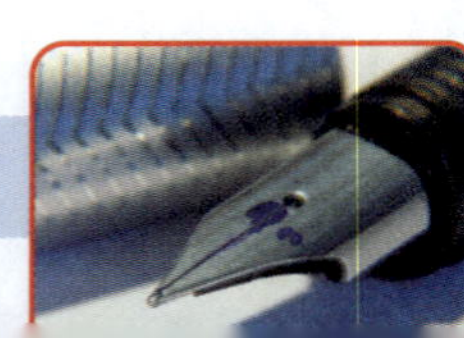

What is this?

1. Complete the drawing. Add the correct word.

What colour is your ...?

1. Ask your friends and write down the colours.
   Start like this:
   What colour is your pencil-case?

object	friend 1	friend 2	me
pencil-case			
schoolbag			
book			

ack 07

Between the lessons

1. Read or listen and draw.

In the classroom there are four pupils.

There is a schoolbag in the dustbin.

On one desk you can see the timetable.

At the door you can see a map.

One boy is sitting on the single desk.

Under one chair there are two books.

On the wall between the board and the door there is a poster with new words.

2. Write your own sentences.
Then complete the drawing.

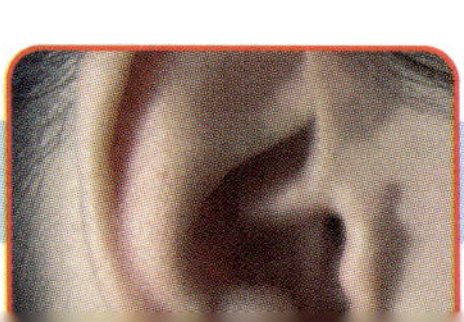

Vocabulary: At school

1. Match the pictures with the correct words. Use your ruler.

a window

a timetable

a book

a chair

a monster

a sharpener

a clock

a pencil-case

a schoolbag

a door

2. Compare with your neighbour. Write the words into the list.

1. ______________________
2. ______________________
3. ______________________
4. ______________________
5. ______________________
6. ______________________
7. ______________________
8. ______________________
9. ______________________
10. ______________________

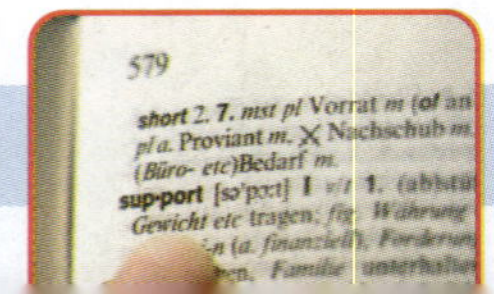

Let us play Bingo

1. Draw nine of these hobbies. Draw each of them in one square.
2. Then listen to the speaker.
   When you have got the named picture, make a cross.
   The one who has got three in a row first calls 'BINGO'!

ck 37

to play computer games

to play basketball

to listen to music

to sing

to play table tennis

to skateboard

to swim

to watch TV

to play soccer

to draw

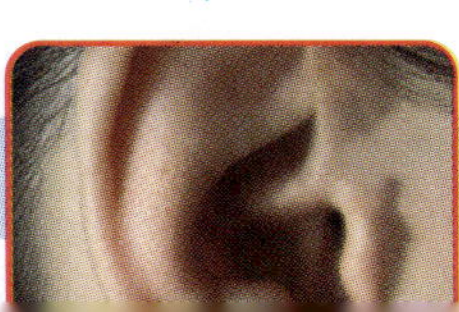

Tom's week

1. Listen to the text on CD and stick in the correct picture cards. You can find the words at page 53. Then stick in the word cards or write.

Track 10

On Monday	Tom		
On Tuesday	he		
On Wednesday	he		
On Thursday	he		
On Friday	he		
On Saturday	he		
On Sunday	he		

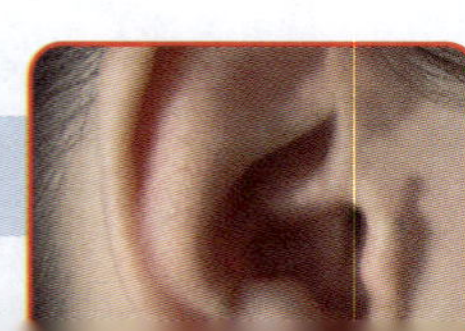

ack 10

Tom's hobbies

1. Listen to the text 'Tom's week'. Tick the right sentence.

	Yes, he does.	No, he does not.
Does Tom play soccer on Monday?		
Does Tom play basketball?		
Does Tom watch TV ?		
Does he listen to music?		
Does Tom like horses?		
Does he go swimming on Tuesday?		
Does Tom rest on Sunday?		
Does Tom go to parties?		

Some more hobbies

2. Match the right cards and draw lines.

to dance

to sing

to play table tennis

to skateboard

to do judo

What are their hobbies?

1. Complete the sentences with **like** or **likes**.
   Use the correct form.

Betty likes to play soccer.

Jim and Sarah ______________ to watch TV.

Robin ______________ to ride a horse.

Linda and John ______________ to play table tennis.

Emily and Paul ______________ to go inline skating.

Marc and Tom ______________ to play basketball.

2. And you?
   What do you like to do?

I ____.

3. And your best friend?
   What does he/she like to do?

He/ She ____.

Interview about hobbies

1. Do your own interview in class. Use ☹ and ☺.
   First, make notes of the hobbies you will ask for.
   Start like this:
   Peter, **do you like** to play computer games?

name	to play computer games	to listen to music	…		
Emily	☺	☺			

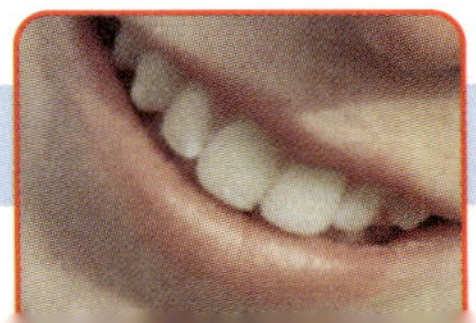

Vocabulary: Free time

1. Match the pictures with the correct words. Use your ruler.

to write

to read

music

a game

to sing

a picture

to swim

a pupils' magazine

a question

soccer

2. Compare with your neighbour. Write the words into the list.

1. ______________________
2. ______________________
3. ______________________
4. ______________________
5. ______________________
6. ______________________
7. ______________________
8. ______________________
9. ______________________
10. ______________________

mit dem Wörterbuch arbeiten

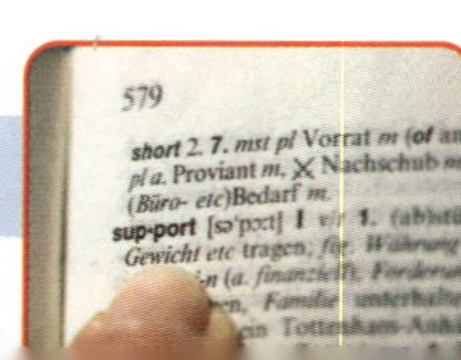

Christmas

1. Decorate the Christmas tree.
   Cut out the Christmas tree decoration on page 55.
   Stick it onto the tree.

2. Present your design to the class.

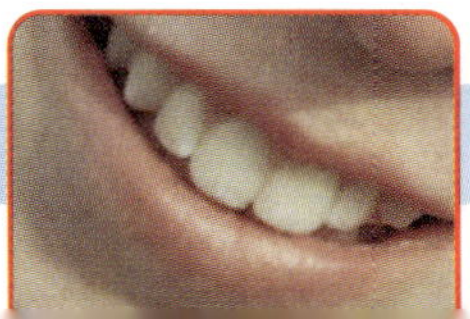

Decorations and reading

1. What all do you use to decorate your home at Christmas?
   Make a list. Use a dictionary if you need to.

To decorate our home at Christmas, we use

– a ______________________________

– ______________________________

– ______________________________

– ______________________________

2. Which sentences can you use for a Christmas card?
   Tick the boxes.

☐ Dear

☐ How are you?

☐ Easter was fun.

☐ Please come to my birthday.

☐ Have a lovely Christmas.

☐ Good bye!

☐ Regards from ______________

3. Can you imagine what the sentences mean?
   Talk about the meaning in class.

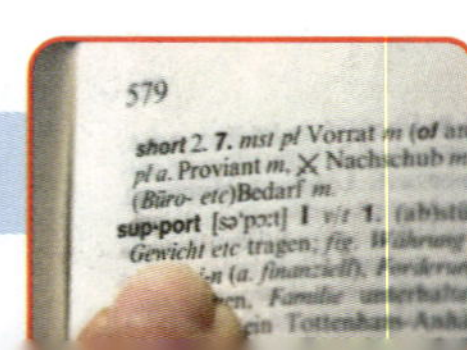

Easter

1. You are the artist.
   Colour the Easter egg.

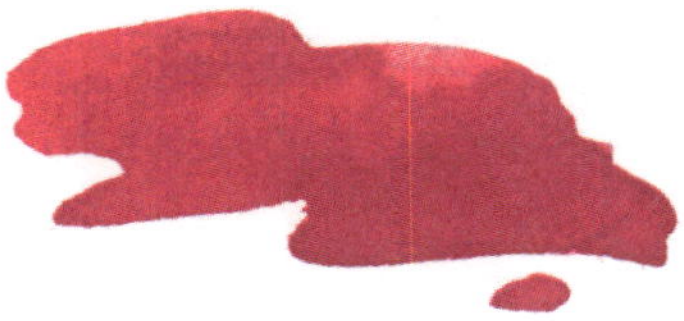

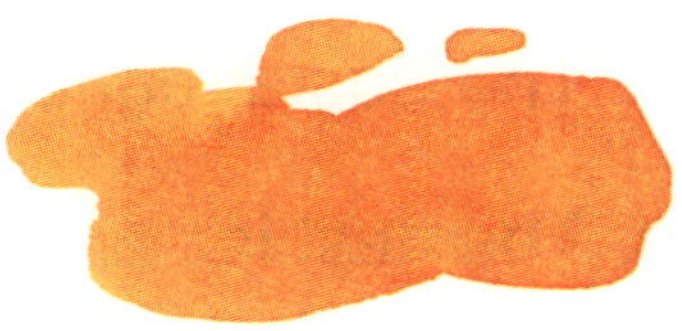

2. Present your design to the class.
   Say which colours you used:

To colour my Easter egg I used ____________________.

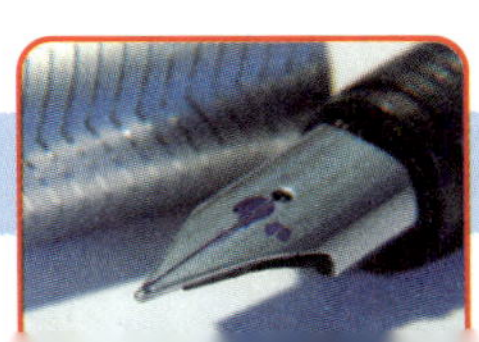

Where is ...?

1. Look at the picture.
   Describe where these objects are.
   Complete the text below the picture.

2. Now complete the text.
   Fill in the correct preposition.

a. The chocolate is ____on____ *(~~under~~ / on)* the table.

b. The Easter bunny is ________ *(beside / under)* the couch.

c. The Easter eggs are ________ *(in / in front of)* the nest.

d. The nest is ________ *(on / behind)* the lamp.

e. The presents are ________ *(in / under)* the cupboard.

Vocabulary: Around the year

1. Match the pictures with the correct words. Use your ruler.

a candle

an Easter bunny

an egg

a present

a stocking

a Christmas tree

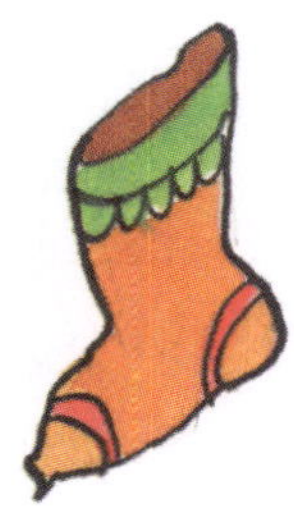

2. Compare with your neighbour. Write the words into the list.

1. ______________________
2. ______________________
3. ______________________
4. ______________________
5. ______________________
6. ______________________

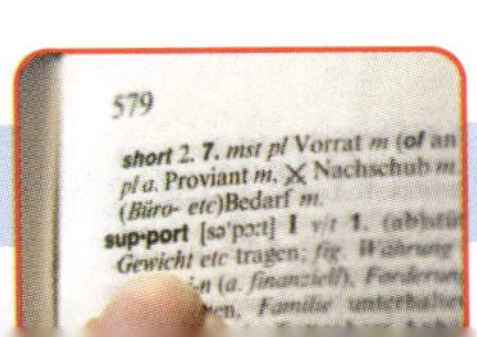

Mein Sprachenportfolio

Über mich

Name: ______________________________

Geburtstag: ______________________________

Geburtsort: ______________________________

Geburtsland: ______________________________

Geschwister: ______________________________

Hobbys: ______________________________

Haustiere: ______________________________

Foto einkleben oder Bild malen

Ich kann folgende Sprachen verstehen:

____

____

Ich spreche diese Sprachen mit meiner Familie:

____

____

Mit meinen Freunden spreche ich:

____

____

In der Schule habe ich bereits folgende Sprachen gelernt:

____

____

Diese Sprachen möchte ich gerne noch lernen:

____

____

In diesen Ländern, in denen eine andere Sprache als Deutsch gesprochen wird, war ich schon einmal:

____

____

Name: ______________________ Datum: ____________

Ich kenne englische Wörter zu diesen Themen:

- ☐ Zahlen
- ☐ Farben
- ☐ Wetter
- ☐ Tiere
- ☐ Schule
- ☐ Essen und Trinken
- ☐ Körper
- ☐ Kleidung
- ☐ Familie
- ☐ Hobbys
- ☐ ______________
- ☐ Geburtstag
- ☐ Ostern
- ☐ Halloween
- ☐ Weihnachten
- ☐ Jahreszeiten
- ☐ Wochentage
- ☐ Monate
- ☐ Uhrzeit
- ☐ Länder
- ☐ London
- ☐ ______________

Das gefällt mir besonders gut beim Lernen einer Fremdsprache:

- ☐ Lieder
- ☐ Reime und Gedichte
- ☐ Spiele
- ☐ Theater und Rollenspiele
- ☐ Lesen
- ☐ Schreiben
- ☐ Sprechen
- ☐ mit Sprache spielen
- ☐ über Sprache nachdenken
- ☐ etwas über andere Länder erfahren
- ☐ ______________________
- ☐ ______________________

Name: ______________________ Datum: ____________

Was ich schon kann

Das hat mir in Kapitel 1 'Welcome to English' am meisten Spaß gemacht:

____

____

____

Das sind meine englischen Lieblingswörter und -sätze:

____

____

____

____

____

____

Was ich schon auf Englisch verstehen oder sagen kann, kreuze ich an:

☐ Ich kann englisch klingende Wörter in meiner Umgebung (z. B. in Zeitschriften, im Supermarkt, im TV) erkennen.

☐ Ich kenne Länder, in denen Englisch gesprochen wird.

Was ich schon kann

Das hat mir in Kapitel 2 'About me' am meisten Spaß gemacht:

____

____

____

Das sind meine englischen Lieblingswörter und -sätze:

____

____

____

____

____

Was ich schon auf Englisch verstehen oder sagen kann, kreuze ich an:

- ☐ Ich kann jemanden begrüßen.
- ☐ Ich kenne die Zahlen von 1 bis 12.
- ☐ Ich kann sagen, wie ich heiße.
- ☐ Ich kann sagen, wie alt ich bin.
- ☐ Ich kann sagen, woher ich komme.
- ☐ Ich kann jemanden vorstellen.

So merke ich mir englische Wörter:

____

____

Name: ______________________ Datum: ____________

Was ich schon kann

Das hat mir in Kapitel 3 'At school' am meisten Spaß gemacht:

____

____

____

Was ich schon auf Englisch verstehen oder sagen kann, kreuze ich an:

☐ Ich kann meine Lieblingsfarbe nennen.
☐ Ich kenne die Wochentage.
☐ Ich kann fragen, ob jemand etwas besitzt.
☐ Ich kann sagen, wo etwas liegt.

Wörter, die ich auf Englisch zu den Themen *Farben, Wochentage, Schulsachen* kenne:

Name: ______________________ Datum: __________

Was ich schon kann

Das hat mir in Kapitel 4 'Free time' am meisten Spaß gemacht:

____

____

____

Das sind meine englischen Lieblingswörter und -sätze:

____

____

____

____

____

____

Was ich schon auf Englisch verstehen oder sagen kann, kreuze ich an:

- ☐ Ich kann den „What about you"-Rap verstehen und mitsprechen.
- ☐ Ich kann sagen, was ich gerne mache.
- ☐ Ich kann jemanden fragen, welche Sportarten und Hobbys er mag.

Darauf achte ich, wenn ich ein Interview mache:

____

____

Name: ______________________ Datum: ____________

Was ich schon kann

Das hat mir in Kapitel 10a 'Around the year' am meisten Spaß gemacht:

____

____

____

Was ich schon auf Englisch verstehen oder sagen kann, kreuze ich an:

- ☐ Ich kann das Lied 'Jingle Bells' mitsingen.
- ☐ Ich kenne Weihnachtstraditionen aus verschiedenen Ländern.

Wörter, die ich auf Englisch zu den Themen *Weihnachten* und *Ostern* kenne:

Mein Schatz

- Fotos aus dem Englischunterricht
- Englisches aus Zeitungen und Prospekten
- E-Mails und Post
- Geschichten, zu denen ich gemalt oder geschrieben habe
- Spiele, die mir gefallen haben
- Kassetten, die ich besprochen habe
- Lieder, die ich singen kann
- Bild-Wort-Collagen
- Gedichte und Reime, die ich kennen gelernt habe
- Lieblingswörter und -sätze
- … und vieles mehr

4. Free time: p. 24: Tom's week

plays soccer.

goes swimming.

watches TV.

listens to music.

reads a comic.

rests.

goes to a party.

5. Around the year: p. 29: Christmas

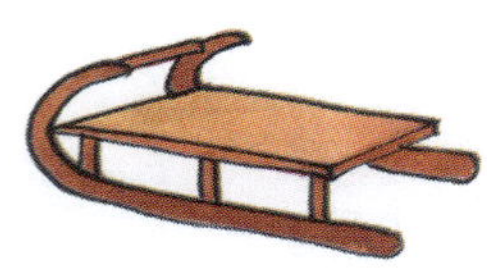